**DATE DUE**

| | | | | | |
|---|---|---|---|---|---|
| | | | | | |
| | | | | | |
| | | | | | |
| | | | | | |
| | | | | | |
| | | | | | |
| | | | | | |
| | | | | | |
| | | | | | |

DEMCO, INC. 38-3012

# Victoria

# Romantic
# Touches

# Victoria

# *Romantic Touches*

## Charming Handmade Projects for Every Room

### GILLIAN HASLAM

HEARST BOOKS
A Division of Sterling Publishing Co., Inc.
New York

DEDICATION

*For Richard and my family, with love*

Library of Congress Cataloging-in-Publication Data
Victoria romantic touches : charming handmade projects for every room.
     p. cm.
  Includes index.
  ISBN 1-58816-409-8
1. House furnishings. 2. Interior decoration accessories. 3. Decoration and ornament—Victorian style.
  TT387.V53 2004
  745.5—dc22

               2004007385

10  9  8  7  6  5  4  3  2  1

Published by Hearst Books
A Division of Sterling Publishing Co., Inc.
387 Park Avenue South, New York, N.Y. 10016

Hearst Books is proud to continue the superb style, quality, and tradition of Victoria magazine with every book we publish. On our beautifully illustrated pages you will always find inspiration and ideas about the subjects you love.

Victoria is a trademark owned by Hearst Magazines Property, Inc., in USA, and Hearst Communications, Inc., in Canada. Hearst Books is a trademark owned by Hearst Communications, Inc.

Distributed in Canada by Sterling Publishing c/o Canadian Manda Group,
One Atlantic Avenue, Suite 105, Toronto, Ontario, Canada M6K 3E7

Distributed in Australia by Capricorn Link (Australia) Pty. Ltd.
P.O. Box 704, Windsor, NSW 2756, Australia

Printed in China

ISBN 1-58816-409-8

Designed by Christine Wood
Illustrations by Kate Simunek

# contents

# introduction

Turning a house into a home is all about personalizing it, about moving away from the uniformity of mass-produced home furnishings and styling the rooms with special touches to reflect your individuality.

In this book, we have gathered together a stylish collection of projects to help you add your own touch to the living room, the bedroom, and the dining room. All the projects are easy to sew and many only require the simplest of skills—if you can stitch a straight seam, then you can manage these ideas. Many of the projects just use a small amount of fabric, so you can change the look of a room simply by adding a few new pillows or a seat cover. And if you're not inclined to make the projects completely from scratch, you can even use some of the design ideas to embellish ready-made furnishings, such as decorating a store-bought pillow cover or trimming a plain headboard with bands of colored silky ribbons.

Whether you want to turn plain kitchen chairs into something special, bring a touch of sheer luxury to your bedroom, dress your windows with stylish drapes, update your sofa with the classiest of pillows, make scented sachets for your closet, or add glamour to your dining table, you will find the perfect solution in this book.

chapter one

# pillows and
# curtains

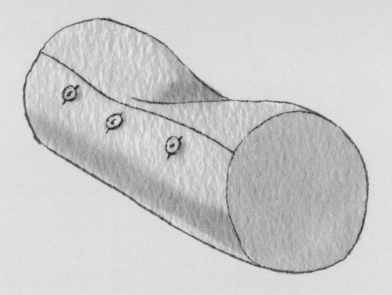

# cream bolster pillow

This comfortingly plump bolster pillow is made from unbleached muslin and provides the perfect foil for the bright pinks, yellows, and oranges of the pillows it accompanies. When using bright colors such as these, it's a good idea to add a few touches of cool, solid-color fabrics to provide contrast and to prevent the rich color scheme from becoming overwhelming. The rounded shape of this bolster complements the pleasing curves of the chair and footstool.

## YOU WILL NEED

**Unbleached muslin**

**Bolster pillow form**

**Tape measure**

**Scissors**

**Pins**

**Sewing machine, with buttonhole attachment**

**Needle and thread**

**Three large cream buttons**

## TIP

Rather than using plain buttons, you could cover buttons to match the fabric. Simply buy a button-covering kit, available from most fabric or craft stores.

1 Cut a piece of fabric measuring the length of the bolster plus 1-in for seams, and the circumference of the bolster plus 3-in.

2 Fold, pin, press, and stitch a ½-in hem along the two sides of the bolster fabric. Turn one of the hemmed edges over by 2-in, wrong sides facing, and pin together. Mark the position of the three buttonholes with pins. Stitch the buttonholes.

3 Snip the
buttonholes open.
Overlapping the fabric by 2-in, mark the button
positions with pins and sew the three buttons in
place on the underlap. Button the fabric to make
an open-ended tube (you could also pin the fabric
to hold it in place). Snip around each end at ½-in
intervals, making each cut no more than ⅜-in deep.
Turn wrong side out.

4 Cut two circles of fabric for the ends,
adding a ½-in seam allowance all around. Right
sides facing (you need to turn the tube inside
out), pin the ends to the buttoned tube, and
stitch together. Unbutton the cover and turn it
right side out. Place the bolster pillow form
inside the cover, and button the cover.

# ribbon-tied pillow

Using a grommet kit, available from fabric or craft stores, provides a quick and simple way to add decoration to a plain pillow cover. Here, a navy blue cotton pillow cover has been embellished with a pretty ribbon that crisscrosses its way down the pillow and is tied in a neat bow at the base. It's also easy to change the ribbon if you alter the decoration of your room.

## YOU WILL NEED

Fabric for pillow cover

Scissors

Pins

Sewing machine and thread

Grommet kit

Ribbon

12-in pillow form

## TIP

Instead of making the pillow cover,
you could punch grommet
holes in a store-bought cover
and thread the ribbon through.

1 For the pillow front, cut a
piece of fabric 13 x 17-in. To create the pleat
in the fabric behind the ribbon, lay the fabric flat,
right side up. Measure in 5-in from one short edge and
fold the fabric back by 1-in. Measure along another 3-in,
then fold the fabric back by 1-in. Pin and baste these
folds. This fabric will now form a 13-in square, and
there will be a 1-in gap between the folds.

2 Mark the positions of the
grommets with pins. Each grommet should be 1½-in away
from the edge of the fold. Make the first pair 2-in down
from the top edge of the fabric, then leave a 3-in gap
between subsequent pairs. Following the instructions on
the kit, insert the grommets.

3 The back of the pillow has an envelope opening. Cut two rectangles of fabric, each 13 x 9-in. Fold, pin, and stitch a ½-in hem on one long edge of each rectangle. Overlap the two rectangles by 4-in, with the hemmed edges facing inward.

4 Pin and baste the overlapping pieces together just inside the top and bottom seamlines. This will make a 13-in square.

5 Place the front and back together, right sides facing. Pin all around, and stitch a ½-in seam. Trim the seam and corners. Remove the basting from the back and turn right side out.

6 Lace the ribbon through the grommets (lacing horizontally on the underside and diagonally on top); tie in a bow. Trim the ends, then stitch a narrow hem at each end. Insert the pillow form. Remove the basting holding the pleat in place.

# organdy pillow

This delicate organdy pillow would look extremely elegant displayed on a bedroom chair or sitting atop a pile of crisp linen-covered pillows. It would make a perfect gift as you can choose the monogram to suit the recipient. Instead of using pearly seed beads, you could embroider a name or short message on the front.

## YOU WILL NEED

**Pattern paper**

**Organdy**

**Ruler**

**Scissors**

**Pins**

**Sewing machine**

**Needle and thread**

**Batting**

**Tailor's chalk**

**Pearl seed beads**

### TIP

Instead of filling the pillow with batting, you could use tiny dried rosebuds or lavender to make a scented sachet.

1 Make a pattern for the border, which has corners with diagonal folds, known as miters. On pattern paper draw two parallel lines each 8-in long and 4-in apart. Draw a fold line halfway between them, extending 2-in beyond them at each end. Draw diagonal lines from the ends of the outer lines to the fold line. Add a ½-in seam allowance all around and cut out the pattern. Pin the pattern to the organdy and cut out. Repeat to cut four border pieces in total.

2 Pin two of the borders' pointed ends together, right sides facing. Stitch a ½-in seam, pivoting at the point and stopping ½-in from each edge. Attach the other two borders in the same way, so all the pointed ends are joined, forming one continuous band. Trim the seams and corners, and turn right side out.

3 With the top and underneath miters aligned, press the miters and the folded edges from the right side at each corner. Turn under, pin, and press a ½-in hem on each raw edge of the border.

4 Cut two 9-in squares of organdy for the front and back of the pillow. Place together and slip between the pressed hems of the border. Pin and stitch all around, leaving a small gap. Fill the pillow with batting and stitch the gap closed.

5 Cut a 5-in square of organdy. Fold under, pin, and stitch the narrowest possible hem all around. Using tailor's chalk, draw the monogram in the center of the square. Sew the seed beads on one at a time, following the outline.

6 Attach this square to the front of the pillow with a few stitches at each of the four corners, then add a single seed bead to each corner.

# double-layer pillow cover

The combination of an under layer of pale pink cotton and a gauzy, floating organdy top layer makes this pillow cover look extremely feminine and sophisticated. The crisp edging emphasizes the contrast between the two fabrics. A row of these pillows in a variety of sugared almond colors—the palest of greens, yellows, pinks, and blues—would look perfect lined up on a white sofa.

## YOU WILL NEED

**Pale pink cotton fabric**

**Tape measure**

**Scissors**

**Pins**

**Sewing machine and thread**

**Organdy**

**Rectangular pillow form,
12 x 18-in**

## TIP

A simple "envelope style" back
avoids the need to fit zippers to
such delicate fabric.

1 To make the pink cover,
cut a piece of fabric for the
front 13 x 19-in. For the back,
cut two pieces, each 13 x 12-in.
Fold over, pin, and stitch a ½-in
hem on one of the long edges of each back piece. Lay the front
piece right side up. Place the two back pieces on top, right side
down and with the hemmed edges overlapping so that the raw
edges align with those of the front. Pin around all four sides.
Stitch a ½-in seam all around. Trim the seam and corners, and
turn the cover right side out.

2 For the organdy
back, cut two pieces
14 x 12-in. Fold, pin,
press, and stitch a ½-in
hem on one of the long edges of each back piece. Overlap the two
hemmed edges to form a rectangle 14 x 20-in and pin the
overlapping pieces together. Fold, pin, and press a ½-in hem all
around.

3 For the organdy front, cut
a piece 22 x 28-in. At each corner, measure in 5-in
along each edge and then fold in these corner
triangles toward the center. Cut ¼-in outside each
fold line to remove the corner triangles leaving ¼-in
seam allowances.

4 With ¼-in still folded in on each corner, find the
halfway point and mark it with a pin. Fold the
organdy between the pins to form the double layer of
edging, with diagonal folds at the corners. Press.

5 With the mitered side of the
organdy front facing upward, center
the organdy back over it, right side
up. The back will cover the raw edges
of the front. Pin all around, and
stitch close to the edge of the back.

6 Slipstitch the diagonal
folds on the mitered corners
together (by taking the
needle through the folds
alternately, with tiny stitches
in between). Place the pillow
form inside the pink cover,
then slip that inside the
organdy cover, with the
openings at the back.

# white lace pillow

This old-fashioned pillow cover is made from a piece of antique embroidered cotton, edged with a soft ruffle of matching cotton lace edging. This design is a good way to breathe new life into a damaged piece of fabric, as the pillow cover is pieced together like an easy form of patchwork. Here it is made with four large squares cut diagonally on the fabric, with a smaller central square.

## YOU WILL NEED

Embroidered cotton fabric

Tape measure

Scissors

Pins

Sewing machine,
or needle and thread

White backing fabric

Cotton lace edging

12-in pillow form

TIP

If you only have smaller pieces of
fabric to work with, you could
create a similar effect by piecing
strips together in the style of log
cabin patchwork.

1 Cut four squares of
embroidered fabric, each
7 x 7-in. If you are using a
fabric with a horizontal
pattern, such as here, you
need to make sure all
pieces feature the same portion of the
pattern—it may be easiest to cut four pieces of
paper to the correct size and place them on the
fabric first, to ensure the patterns run in the
right direction.

2 Pin two squares together,
right sides facing, taking a ½-in
seam allowance and making sure the horizontal
patterns run at right angles to each other. Pin the
other two squares in the same way, then open out
the pinned pieces to double-check they will marry
up correctly.

3 Sew along the two pinned seams, so you have two rectangles. Press the seams open. Pin the two long edges of the rectangles together, open them up to check that the patterns run in the right direction, then sew together to form the pillow front. Press the seam open.

4 Cut a square of embroidered fabric 2 x 2-in. As this forms the center of the pillow, you may be able to use an embroidered motif if one appears on your fabric. Fold and press a ¼-in hem on all sides. Place the square diagonally over the center of the pillow, pin, and stitch in place.

5 For the back of the pillow, cut two pieces of backing fabric 9 x 13-in. Fold over a ½-in hem on one longer side of each rectangle; pin, press, and stitch. Overlap the two rectangles by 4-in, with the hemmed edges toward the center. This should make a square the same size as the pillow front. Pin together through the overlap.

6 On the right side of the pillow back, pin the lace around the edge, with the ruffle pointing inward. Allow extra fullness at the corners. At one corner, stitch the two ends together and press the seam open. Place the pillow front on top, right side down. Pin, sandwiching the ruffle in between. Stitch a ½-in seam around all four sides. Remove all the pins, turn right side out, press and insert the pillow form through the opening in the back.

# contrast-bordered pillow

Crisp white cotton partnered with a small-scale blue-and-white checked fabric is always a winning combination. A row of three neat ties, made from the contrasting border fabric, is used to secure the opening. The instructions given here are for a square pillow cover, but the design would work equally well as a pillow sham.

## YOU WILL NEED

Pattern paper

Ruler

Scissors

White cotton fabric

Pins

Sewing machine and thread

Checked fabric

12-in pillow form

## TIP

There are numerous ways to close envelope openings. You could use checked or plain ribbons, delicate pearly buttons, or buttons covered in the checked fabric.

1 First, make a pattern for the border, which has corners with diagonal folds, known as miters. On pattern paper draw two parallel lines each 13-in long and 5-in apart. Draw a fold line between these two lines, extending 2½-in beyond the original lines at each end. Draw diagonal lines from the ends of the outer lines to the fold line. Add a ½-in seam allowance all around and cut out the pattern. Pin the pattern to the checked fabric and cut out. Repeat to cut four border pieces in total.

2 Pin two of the borders' pointed ends together, right sides facing. Stitch a ½-in seam, pivoting at the point and stopping ½-in from each edge. Attach the other two borders in the same way, to form a continuous band. Trim the ends and corners, and turn right side out. With the top and underneath miters aligned, press the miters and the folded edges from the right side at each corner. Baste the two layers together along the raw edges.

3 For the pillow back, cut a 13-in square of white cotton. For the pillow front, cut two rectangles of white cotton: one 13 x 5-in, the other 13 x 11-in. Turn under, pin, and stitch a ½-in hem down one of the long sides of each rectangle. Overlap these rectangles as shown, to form a 13-in square. Pin and baste the overlap together just inside the top and bottom seamlines. On both the front and back, turn under a 1/2-in hem all around, pin, and press.

4 Place the pillow back and front with wrong sides facing, edges even, and pin them together 2-in from the outer edges. Slip the inner edges of the mitered border between the front and back pieces. Pin and stitch all around close to the edge of the white cotton.

5 To make the ties, cut six rectangles of checked fabric, each 1-in wide and 8-in long. Fold in half lengthwise, wrong sides facing. Turn in the raw edges on the long side and the ends. Pin, press, and topstitch. Tie a small knot at one end of each. One tie of each pair will be sewn to the underlap and the other to the overlap of the opening.

6 Mark the position of the three pairs of ties with pins, then stitch the ties in place. Insert the pillow form and tie the bows.

# paneled pillow

This is an excellent way of making a little go a long way. A small remnant of fabric, left over from making curtains for this living room, has been used as a central panel on a pillow cover. This technique works best with fabrics with a strong motif or pattern and is a good way of linking soft furnishings.

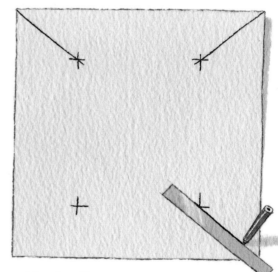

**YOU WILL NEED**

**Fabric remnant with a strong motif**

**Fabric for the surround**

**Scissors**

**Pattern paper**

**Ruler**

**Fabric for the border and back**

**Bias binding to match the pillow cover fabric (see step 5)**

**Piping cord**

**Zipper**

**Sewing machine and thread**

**Pins**

**Pillow form**

**TIP**

If you wish, you could stitch this panel, with or without the border, to a store-bought pillow cover.

1 Cut out the central motif for your pillow (here, a rectangle has been cut). Next, cut a piece of fabric for the surround—this should be at least 2-in wider and deeper than the motif. Cut a paper pattern for the central hole in the surround fabric—here it was easiest to draw a rectangle then soften the corners with curves. Place this pattern on the surround fabric and cut out the hole. Turn the raw edges under by ½-in, snipping into the seam allowance on the curved portions, and pin in place on top of the motif fabric. Slipstitch in place (see page 25, step 6).

2 To complete the pillow front, make a pattern for the four pieces of border. First, cut out a piece of paper the size of your pillow. Place the front panel on top of this, positioned centrally, and mark the corners of the panel on the paper. Draw diagonal lines from these four marks to the outer corners of the pillow. Label the areas for the two sides, the top, and the bottom pieces, then cut out the pattern pieces.

3 Cut out one piece of fabric for each pattern piece, adding ½-in all around for seam allowances. Pin two adjoining pieces together along the diagonal lines, right sides facing. Stitch, stopping ½-in from the inner edge. Add the third and fourth pieces in the same way. From the same fabric, cut a piece for the back, adding a ½-in seam allowance all around.

4 Fold under a ½-in seam on the inner edges, pin, and press. Position over the central panel and pin in place. Stitch around all four sides close to the edge. Press the seams flat.

5 To make the bias binding for the piping, cut a strip of fabric on the bias (diagonal), long enough to go around the pillow, plus 1-in, and wide enough to wrap around the cord, plus 1-in. If you need to join lengths of fabric, join them on the diagonal, as shown. For the piping, wrap the fabric around the cord, right side out, then machine stitch as close to the cord as possible, using the piping foot.

6 Place the pillow front right side up. Pin and then baste the piping all around, with the seam allowance pointing outward; clip

into the seam allowance at the corners. Place the zipper at the bottom, face down, with the teeth just covering the edge of the piping. Pin. Using the zipper foot, stitch the bottom tape in place, close to the teeth.

7 Turn over the zipper, turning under the seam allowance. Turn under and press the seam allowance at the bottom of the back

piece. With the back right side up, and the folded edge butting up to the folded edge of the front, pin the back to the other zipper tape. Topstitch alongside the teeth and across the ends of the zipper as far as the fold. Open the zipper. Place the front and back with right sides facing. Pin and stitch a ½-in seam on the remaining edges. Trim Corners. Turn right side out, press, and insert the pillow form.

# bejeweled tieback

Curtain tiebacks offer such a simple solution to changing your window dressing. While it can be expensive and time-consuming to make new drapes, simply changing the tiebacks allows you to coordinate different colors or fabrics within a room, linking various elements within the décor. This striking tieback creates a decorative focal point in its own right.

## YOU WILL NEED

Pattern paper

Tape measure or ruler

Scissors

Fabric

Stiff interfacing

Pins

Sewing machine

Needle and thread

Decorative ornaments

Two small curtain rings

Small wall hook

## TIP

Before cutting the fabric, pin the paper pattern in place around the curtain to check that the tieback is long enough to hold the curtain in place without gathering up the fabric too tightly.

1 For a crescent-shaped tieback, fold the pattern paper in half and draw a half-crescent from the fold line outward, adding a ½-in seam allowance all around; cut out the pattern and unfold so you have a symmetrical shape. For a rectangular tieback, cut out a rectangle of the appropriate size from the pattern paper, allowing for a ½-in seam allowance all around. Place the pattern on the curtain fabric and cut out two pieces. Cut one piece of interfacing, without the seam allowance.

2 Lay the interfacing over the wrong side of one of the pieces of tieback fabric, so the fabric seam allowance forms an even margin all the way around. Fold the seam allowance over the interfacing and pin in place. Cut notches in the seam allowance to allow the fabric to lie flat against the interfacing. Press. Baste together and remove the pins.

3 Fold in the seam allowance on the second piece of fabric, cutting notches as in step 2. Press, then place on top of the interfacing, right side up, and pin in place. Slipstitch around the edges (see page 25, step 6), and remove the basting stitches.

4 Sew the ornaments in place around the upper and lower edges. Sew a curtain ring to each end of the tieback, and fit a hook to the wall.

# linen curtain

Cream linen drapes always look supremely stylish, and their simplicity means you can partner them with almost any style of home furnishings. This curtain could either be made from a length of specially purchased linen, or as a way to reuse an old linen sheet if you are lucky enough to have one. Ideal for summer months, linen window treatments allow light into the room, yet cut out the glare of the sun. Simple ribbon ties and an integral valance provide a fresh and pretty top treatment.

## YOU WILL NEED

Linen

Tape measure

Scissors

Pins

Sewing machine,
or needle and thread

Deep eyelet lace, enough to fit
the width of the curtain

Cream ribbon

Curtain pole and rings

1 Measure the depth of
the window. You will need
this amount of linen, plus
an extra 12-in, or more if you wish to make overlong
curtains (see tip). Rather than joining widths of linen to
make wide curtains, it is better to make two or more
curtains of single widths of fabric as this avoids the need for
bulky seams.

## TIP

These curtains look even better
if made extra long, so they fall in
a puddle on the floor below
the window.

2 Fold over and pin
a double ½-in hem at
one end of the linen and
stitch in place.

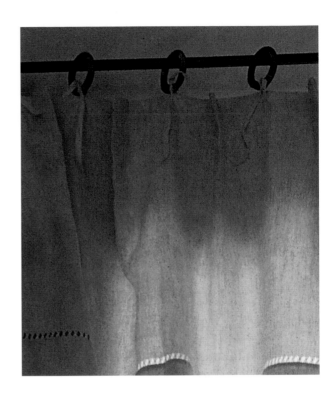

3 Fold over and pin a single ¼-in hem at the other end of the linen. Pin the eyelet lace along this hem as shown, then stitch in place.

4 Fold the top 12-in of the curtain to the front, and press along this line. Cut the cream ribbon into 8-in lengths. Fold the ribbons in half and pin at 6-in intervals along the top of the curtain (or to match the number of curtain rings). Sew securely in place through the fold line, then tie the curtain to the curtain rings.

# window screen

A screen placed in front of a window is an elegantly tailored alternative to a curtain or shade. The trick is to choose a fine fabric that will allow light through, yet still provide privacy. Here a fine voile patterned with colorful butterflies has been used—when bright sunshine pours through the window, the butterflies will appear to be hovering in the air. Organdy (either plain or with an embroidered pattern) would also work well, and in winter you could replace the sheer fabric with panels of velvet to create instant warmth.

## YOU WILL NEED

**Screen frame**
**Sheer fabric**
**Tape measure**
**Scissors**
**Sewing machine and thread**
**Pins**
**Ribbon**

### TIP

This frame has pairs of metal bars through which the fabric panels can slide. Alternatively, you could sew additional ties to the sides and base of the fabric to hold it to the frame, or use a staple gun to attach the fabric to a wooden frame.

1 Measure the width and height of each panel. For each, cut out a piece of fabric measuring twice the width, plus 1½-in, by the height, plus 1½-in.

2 Fold the fabric in half lengthwise, right sides facing. Pin together, and stitch a ¾-in seam around the top and side. Trim the corners.

3 Turn right side out, and
press. Turn under and press
¾-in along the bottom edges;
slipstitch the bottom closed
(see page 25, step 6).

4 Cut two 12-in lengths of ribbon. Fold in
half and stitch each to one of the top corners,
through the center fold on the ribbon. Feed the
fabric through the bars on the frame and tie the
top corners to the frame. Trim the ribbon ends
on the diagonal to prevent raveling.

chapter two

# chair covers

# striped
# cushion pads

Pink candy-stripes on a fresh white background bring a modern,
informal touch to this serene dining room decorated in cool shades
of gray and white. Armed with a staple gun, you can easily give
dining chairs with drop-in seats an instant facelift with new fabric
covers. When using a strong pattern such as this, the most important
thing is to cut and position the fabric so that the stripes are central
and all seats display the same area of pattern. Unless the existing
seats are very worn or the fabric is very thick, you can usually lay the
new fabric over the old.

**YOU WILL NEED**

Scrap fabric, to make
a template

Pins

Scissors

Fabric

Staple gun

**TIP**

Make sure the fabric you choose
for seat covers is reasonably
hardwearing and can be sponged
down if spillages occur.

1 To remove the seat pad, turn the dining chair upside down and look at the fixings. On some chairs you can simply tap hard on the base of the seat and the pad will pop out; on other chairs you may need to use a screwdriver to release holding screws.
Using the scrap fabric, make a template. Pin the scrap fabric tightly over the seat pad and cut out, adding a 3-in allowance all around.

2 Place the template on the fabric and decide where you want the pattern to appear. Cut out the fabric.

3 Place the fabric over the seat pad, pulling the fabric taut, and stab a few pins through to the pad to hold the fabric in position.

4 Turn the pad over and staple the fabric just once in the center of each of the four sides. Turn the pad back again and double-check the pattern is still properly centered and the fabric is pulled tight.

5 Turn the pad face down again and continue stapling. It is best to add a few staples either side of the first four applied in the previous step, and then work into the four corners. Constantly check that the pattern is central and that the fabric is taut. To miter each corner, pull the fabric diagonally over the corner; staple, then fold the excess at each side into a pleat, and staple.

# organdy chair skirt

A gauzy skirt of finest organdy, studded with glistening pearls,
turns an everyday dining chair into the prettiest of seats,
perfect for the boudoir or dressing room. A thin foam pad,
encased in plain white cotton, softens the hard wooden seat,
while tucks along the lower edge add body to the skirt.

## YOU WILL NEED

Pattern paper

Tape measure

Scissors

White cotton fabric

Foam, 1-in thick

Sewing machine

Needle and thread

Organdy

Pearl buttons

## TIP

This style of seat cover works best with lightweight fabric, but a fine cotton lawn could also be used. For the skirt decoration, choose smooth buttons that won't snag stockings.

1 Make a paper pattern of the chair seat adding ½-in seam allowance all around. Cut out two pieces of white cotton to this shape and pin together, right sides facing. Stitch a ½-in seam around the edges, leaving the back edge open. Turn right side out. Use the paper pattern to cut out a piece of foam to the same shape and size, without the seam allowance. Slide the foam into the cotton cover. Turn under and press ½-in on the back edges, and slipstitch the opening closed (see page 25, step 6).

2 Cut out the piece of organdy for the seat, using the same paper pattern and adding a ½-in seam allowance all around. Measure around the front and sides of the seat. Cut a rectangular piece of organdy 1½ times this measurement and 15-in deep to make a 9-in-deep skirt. Turn under and press a double ½-in hem on the two side edges of the skirt; pin and stitch. Turn under a double 1-in hem on the lower edge; pin, press, and topstitch.

3 On the wrong side, measure 2-in from the bottom and mark with a pin. From this point, fold the fabric down 1-in, then back up on itself; on the right side the resulting tuck should just cover the stitching. Pin and press. With the wrong side up, stitch the tuck to the skirt along the top fold. From the top fold, measure up 1-in on the wrong side and then fold, pin, press, and stitch another tuck, so that the resulting tuck on the right side just covers the previous stitching.

4 Pin the skirt to the organdy seat cover, right sides facing. Start by pinning the two ends in place, then pin the rest of the skirt in place, making small pleats in the skirt at regular intervals so that it fits around the seat. Stitch a ½-in seam.

5 Place the top of the cushion cover against the wrong side of the organdy seat cover. Pin and hand-sew them together around the seat edge on the wrong side. Turn right side out, and stitch the pearl buttons to the skirt in a random pattern.

6 To make each of the two ties, cut a length of organdy 4-in wide and 18-in long. Fold in half lengthwise, right sides facing. Pin and stitch a narrow seam along one short edge and the long edge. Turn right side out. Turn under and press the raw edges, then slipstitch the open end. Fold each tie in half and pin to the cotton cushion cover where it meets the inside of the chair back. Sew firmly in place and tie around the chair back.

# simple slipcovers

These contemporary blue-and-white plaid slipcovers dress up chairs in an instant, and provide the perfect way to coordinate mismatching furniture. The covers are far easier and quicker to make than traditional upholstery—just one length of fabric folds over the back of the chair and continues over the seat. It is held in place with ties at the side. If you are using a fabric with a dominant pattern (such as this bold plaid or a large floral pattern), take time to position the fabric carefully so that the pattern is centered on the chair back and seat.

## YOU WILL NEED

**Tape measure**

**Fabric**

**Pattern paper**

**Scissors**

**Sewing machine and thread**

**Pins**

**Solid-color fabric, for the ties**

## TIP

Make sure the fabric you choose for the ties is not too thick, because after folding and stitching it still needs to be flexible enough to be tied into bows. Alternatively, use lengths of strong ribbon, which can simply be sewn in place after the ends are hemmed to prevent raveling.

1 Using a tape measure, measure the back and the seat of the chair. You need to cut a piece of fabric long enough to cover both sides of the chair back, the seat, and the front of the seat cushion. The fabric should be wide enough to drape over the sides of the seat cushion. It is safest to cut a paper pattern first. As with the chair shown here, you may need to shape the pattern around the chair legs

2 Cut out the paper pattern, adding an extra ½-in all around for hemming. Lay the pattern on the fabric, positioning it so that any dominant pattern is centered on the chair back and seat. Cut out the fabric.

3 Lay the fabric
over the chair to ensure
that it fits. Zigzag stitch
the raw edges. Turn under, pin, press, and stitch
a ½-in hem all around, clipping into the inner
corners within the seam allowance. Place the
slipcover on the chair and mark the position of
the side ties with pins.

4 Each tie is made
from a piece of fabric 8 x 2-in.
Turn under and press ¼-in along
each edge, then fold that in half
lengthwise, wrong sides facing. Press and pin. Stitch
across the top, down the side, and across the bottom.
Stitch the ties firmly in place on the cover, making
sure the position of each tie matches its partner.

# deckchair slings

This is such a quick and easy way to give your deckchairs a facelift for summer. The traditional, sturdy wooden frames often outlast the canvas slings, but it's really very simple to stitch a new sling. You may even wish to revarnish the wooden frame or repaint it in a color to complement the canvas.

## YOU WILL NEED

Tape measure

Strong, preshrunk canvas

Scissors

Pins

Sewing machine, or sturdy
needle and strong thread

Staple gun (optional)

1 Unscrew the top and
bottom horizontal wooden bars
holding the existing canvas in place.
Measure the width and length of the existing
canvas sling. Add hem allowances of 1-in to each
side and 4-in to the top and to the bottom. Cut
out the canvas to this size. Turn under, pin, press,
and stitch a 1-in hem down each side. Then turn
under, pin, press, and stitch a ½-in hem at the top
and bottom.

## TIP

If the deckchair cannot be
dismantled, cut away the old canvas
and use a staple gun to attach the
new sling to the wooden bars.
Some fabric stores sell canvas
woven in special widths especially
for deckchairs, which means there's
no need to hem the sides.

2 To make each channel for the two wooden
bars, measure around the bar and add ½-in to this
measurement. Turn under the fabric, pin, and stitch
the channel in place. Stitch another two or three
lines across the width of the canvas to
make the sling strong enough to
hold an adult.

3 Slide the wooden bars through the channels and reattach to the deckchair frame.

4 A new canvas sling for a footstool can be made in exactly the same way, either by sewing channels for the wooden support bars or by using a staple gun to attach the canvas to the frame.

Chut ... bébé dort ...

Hush ... baby sleeps ...

mes souliers

chapter three

# bed linen and accessories

# fitted headboard cover

This headboard cover simply slips over the existing padded headboard like a snugly fitting sleeve. It's the ideal way to give the bed a whole new look, and you could make two different covers to match both winter and summer drapes. Any leftover fabric could be made into covers for throw pillows for the room.

## YOU WILL NEED

**Tape measure**

**Piping cord**

**Fabric for piping casing**

**Scissors**

**Sewing machine with piping foot and thread**

**Pattern paper**

**Fabric for cover**

1 Calculate how much piping you will need by measuring the sides and top of the headboard and adding 12-in. To cover the piping, cut a strip of fabric on the bias (diagonal) to the same length and wide enough to wrap around the cord with a ¼-in seam allowance. If you need to join lengths of fabric, join them on the diagonal. Wrap the fabric around the cord, right side out, then machine stitch as close as possible to the cord, using the piping foot.

### TIP

If using an expensive fabric for covering the headboard, you could use a plain fabric such as calico for the back if it won't be seen. It's best if this is of a similar weight to the main fabric and you may wish to launder it before cutting out, just in case it shrinks.

2 Measure the height and depth of the headboard, and add ½-in seam allowances all around. If the headboard has a slightly curved top, as in this photo, it is probably best to make a paper pattern before cutting the fabric. If the headboard reaches to the floor, you may need to take any fittings into consideration. As this cover does not include a side gusset, add twice the thickness of any padding on the headboard to the width measurement.

3 Cut out the front and back pieces for the cover. If using a fabric with a dominant pattern, position the pattern carefully on the fabric to avoid cutting through motifs at the top of the headboard.

4 Lay the front piece right side up. Pin piping all around the sides and top, with the corded edge facing inward and the fabric raw edges facing out. Clip into the piping seam allowance at the corners. Baste in place. Lay the back piece on top, right side down, enclosing the piping, and pin in place. Stitch all around the three sides. Fold, pin, press, and stitch a hem around the lower edges, then slip the cover onto the headboard.

# tied
# headboard cover

This is such a quick and easy way to soften the appearance of a metal or wooden bedstead. A length of fabric, chosen to complement the bed linen, is hemmed and draped over the horizontal bar of the headboard. Decorative ribbons at the sides hold the fabric in place and add a pretty finishing touch at the same time. You could easily make a number of these headboard covers, to match each set of bed linen, or use the same fabric for the curtains.

## YOU WILL NEED

**Tape measure**

**Fabric**

**Scissors**

**Pins**

**Sewing machine,
or needle and thread**

**Ribbon**

## TIP

If you like to prop yourself up in bed
to read, make this headboard cover
more comfortable by adding a thick
layer of batting underneath the
fabric, or fold a spare blanket
over the headboard before tying
the cover in place.

1 Measure the width of the
bed frame (you need the length
of the horizontal rail) and add a
hem allowance of 2-in to this
measurement. For the length of
fabric required, measure the
distance from the deck, up over
the top horizontal rail, and then
down to the floor or just below
the mattress (depending on the
desired height of the lower edge) and
add 2-in to this measurement.

2 Cut out the
fabric to this size.
Turn under a double ½-in hem on all
four sides, pin, and press. Stitch.

3 Place the hemmed fabric in position over the headboard. Decide the positions of the ribbon ties and mark the places with pins.

4 Cut the ribbon ties. You can either cut lengths which are just long enough to tie into bows (about 8-in) or cut much longer ribbons for more decorative bows which can drape down to the floor. Pin and then stitch the ribbons in place. Tie into bows, then trim the ends diagonally to prevent fraying.

# beribboned headboard

This is such a simple way to jazz up a plain padded headboard. Bands of good-quality ribbon, in colors chosen to match the bed linen, are stitched across the width of the headboard, while separate bows are sewn to the sides. If you wish to make the headboard cover, follow the directions for the fitted headboard cover on page 70, then simply decorate the front with ribbons before attaching the back piece.

## YOU WILL NEED

Tape measure

Lengths of ribbon, in your
choice of colors

Tailor's chalk (optional)

Pins

Scissors

Needle and thread, to match
the ribbon colors

## TIP

For a quick and easy version of this
project, use strips of fusible web to
permanently bond the ribbon to the
headboard cover, following the
manufacturer's instructions.

1 Decide where you want
the ribbon bands to be
stitched and carefully measure
down from the top of the
headboard, marking where the
top edge of the ribbon should
be stitched, with either pins
or tailor's chalk. It is important
to measure accurately so the ribbons are stitched
horizontally and not at a slight angle. Take into account
the height of the pillows.

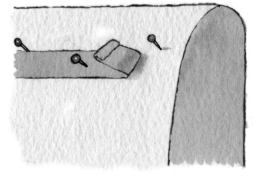

2 Cut the first ribbon
the width of the bedhead
plus the sides and a 1-in
hem. Turn under ½-in at
one end and pin the ribbon
across the headboard, turning under the hem at the other
side. It is probably easiest to "stab" the pins at an angle into
the padding of the headboard. Double-check that the ribbon
is perfectly horizontal. Slipstitch the top of the ribbon in
place (see page 36, step 1), then slipstitch the lower edge.
Repeat with the remaining bands of ribbon.

3 Cut a 24-in length of ribbon to make each bow. Fold a narrow hem at each end and slipstitch. (If you wish, you could cut the ribbon ends on the diagonal before hemming.)

4 Tie each ribbon in a large bow. Pin the bows in place on the sides of the headboard, and sew firmly in place.

# gathered lampshade

A candlestick-style lamp base is given a new lease of life with a softly gathered linen cover which sits on top of the original shade. Here a striped linen has been used and the fabric cut so the white stripe appears as a band toward the bottom of the shade and on the top and bottom edges; if you use a solid-color fabric, you could easily stitch a band of decorative ribbon onto the fabric before gathering it up.

## YOU WILL NEED

Lampshade and base

Tape measure

Scissors

Linen fabric

Pins

Sewing machine,
or needle and thread

Elastic, ¼-in wide

Safety pin

Short length of ribbon

## TIP

Lampshades do have a tendency to collect dust, but as this fabric shade simply slips over the original lampshade, it can easily be removed for laundering.

1 Measure the circumference of the lower, wider edge of the lampshade. Measure down the side of the lampshade to find the depth. Add 8-in to the circumference measurement, and 4-in to the depth measurement. Cut out a rectangle of fabric to this size. If using a striped fabric, remember to position the stripe before cutting out the rectangle.

2 Fold the fabric in half, short ends together and right sides facing. Pin the short ends together, with a seam allowance of ½-in. Stitch the seam, then press it open. You now have a wide tube of fabric with raw edges.

3 With the tube of fabric wrong side out, turn up, pin, press, and sew a double ¼-in hem along one edge. This will be the lower edge of the lampshade.

4 Fold over 2-in of the top edge, pin, and press. Stitch along the lower edge of this folded fabric, and then complete another row of stitching ½-in above this, to create a channel for the elastic.

5 Carefully unpick a few stitches in the side seam by the channel. You need to make a gap just large enough to thread the elastic through.

6 Attach the safety pin to one end of the elastic and use it to feed the elastic all the way through the channel. Pull up the elastic until the cover fits over the shade. Cut off the excess elastic and sew the ends together. Push them inside and hand-sew the opening. Tie the ribbon in a bow and sew it to the gathers.

# dressing table skirt

A full skirt of striped black-and-white fabric is the perfect way to bring this fifties-style, kidney-shaped dressing table right up to date. Simply changing the fabric can give a completely different look to a room—checked gingham would provide a country feel, these stripes give a cool, contemporary look, while a floral-patterned fabric would add a distinctly feminine touch.

## YOU WILL NEED

Tape measure

Scissors

Fabric

Pins

Sewing machine and thread

Staple gun

Ribbon, at least ½-in wide

White craft glue

## TIP

If you are using striped fabric for the skirt, make sure the stripes run in the correct direction before cutting the fabric.

1 Measure around the top edge of the dressing table and double the measurement. Measure the height of the dressing table and add 2-in. Cut out a piece of fabric to this size. Fold under, pin, press, and stitch a 1-in hem on all four sides. Sew a row or two of gathering stitches along the top of the fabric, ½-in from the top, then gently gather up the fabric to fit around the dressing table.

2 Drape the fabric around the dressing table (you could use low-tack tape to hold it in place temporarily). Using the staple gun, attach the two ends to the center back of the table. Adjust the gathers so they fall evenly, then staple the fabric all the way around.

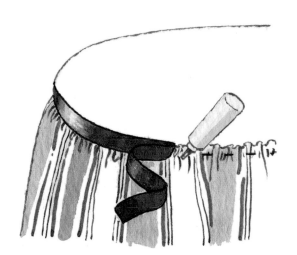

3 Cut a length of ribbon to fit all around the table and carefully glue in place to hide the staples and the gathering stitches.

4 Finally, make a flat ribbon bow and either glue or staple it to the front of the dressing table.

# drawstring scented sachet

This pretty drawstring fabric sachet is perfect for filling with dried rose petals, lavender heads, or mixed potpourri. Hang it either from the headboard to scent the bedroom or inside the closet to add a gentle perfume to clothes. If filled with lavender, it will help keep moths at bay. Replace the potpourri or flower heads as soon as the scent begins to fade.

## YOU WILL NEED

Scissors

Fabric remnants for the bag
and contrasting top edge

Lace edging

Sewing machine, or needle and
thread

Pins

Ribbon

Safety pin

Decorative button

1 Cut out two 4 x 6-in rectangles of fabric for the bag. If you are using a fabric with a dominant motif (as used here), position the motif centrally on each side of the bag. Trim the bottom corners at an angle of 45 degrees, to make the curved bottom.

## TIP

These drawstring sachets could also
be used as giftbags, to enclose
small presents for friends.

2 Pin the pieces of fabric together, right sides facing and with the lace sandwiched between them around the bottom curve as shown. Sew a ½-in seam around the sides and bottom. Press the seams open, turn right side out, and press.

3 Cut two 4 x 3-in rectangles of contrasting fabric for the top edging. Fold, pin, press, and stitch a ½-in hem down each short edge. Fold one fabric piece in half lengthwise, wrong sides facing, and pin it to one half of the bag at the top, enclosing ½-in of the raw edge of the bag. Topstitch in place. Repeat for the other fabric piece.

4 Cut two 4-in lengths of ribbon. Pin one on top of the seam joining the main bag and one contrasting fabric piece, turning under ½-in at each end of the ribbon. Carefully stitch along the top and bottom edges of the ribbon to create a channel for the ribbon drawstring. Leave both ends of the channel open. Attach the second ribbon to the other contrasting fabric piece in the same way.

5 Cut a long length of ribbon for the handle. Attach the safety pin to one end and feed the ribbon through the entire channel, leaving a long loop on each side. Knot the two ends together securely.

6 Sew a decorative button to the ribbon channel, making sure you only sew through the channel and not through the ribbon drawstring.

# shoe sachets

Have you ever splurged more money than you can possibly justify on a pair of must-have dream shoes? To assuage your feelings of guilt, the least you can do is to look after them properly. These scented sachets have tapered ends so you can push them into the toes of your shoes to help them keep their shape, and are filled with lavender to keep them smelling sweet. When the lavender loses its aroma, simply refill the sachet with fresh herbs or potpourri.

## YOU WILL NEED

**Fabric**

**Scissors**

**Tailor's chalk**

**Ruler**

**Pins**

**Sewing machine, or needle and thread**

**Scrap paper**

**Fabric paint**

**Fine paintbrush**

**Dried lavender**

**Ribbon**

## TIP

Use any leftover fabric to make a simple drawstring bag to store the shoes in, to prevent them from getting dusty or becoming scuffed in the closet.

1 For each sachet cut out two rectangles of fabric 8 x 4-in. To make the tapered toe, use tailor's chalk to make a mark halfway down one long side and another mark 1-in in from the corner on one short side. Join the two marks and cut along the line. Repeat on the other side, and use this as a pattern to taper the remaining rectangles.

2 Place the two pieces of fabric together, right sides facing. Pin and stitch a ½-in seam around the sides and toe. Turn over a ½-in hem along the top edge and stitch, using a long, wide zigzag stitch and thread in a contrasting color. Turn right side out.

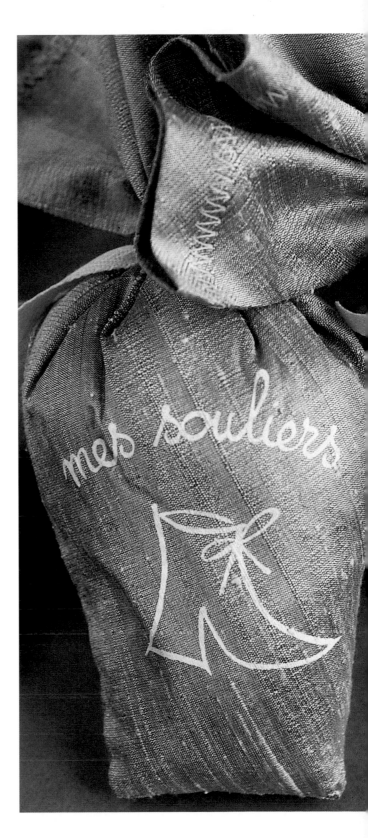

3 Place a piece of scrap paper inside the sachet to prevent the paint from leaking through. Paint your chosen design onto the fabric and leave to dry. (Some fabric paints need to be pressed with a warm iron to fix them—follow the instructions supplied with the paint.) Remove the scrap paper. Alternatively, you could embroider the design.

4 Half-fill the bag with dried lavender, and then tie a length of pretty ribbon tightly around the top to secure.

# initialed
# linen sachets

These charming herb-filled linen sachets would make a perfect gift, and you can personalize them using the recipient's monogram. They are ideal for tucking into closets, drawers, and linen chests, to ward off moths and keep fabrics gently fragranced. The monograms are stamped onto heavyweight linen using a store-bought stamp, but if you wish, you could either paint them freehand or embroider the monogram or name. Small, brightly colored beads are sewn onto each corner as a decorative touch.

## YOU WILL NEED

**Heavyweight linen**

**Ruler**

**Scissors**

**Initial stamp**

**Fabric paint**

**Fine paintbrush**

**Scrap paper**

**Small beads**

**Pins**

**Sewing machine,
or needle and thread**

**Batting**

**Dried scented herbs**

## TIP

Instead of beads at the corners, you could add an edging of eyelet lace. Simply sandwich it between the two layers in step 3, with the lace edge facing inward.

1 Cut two squares of linen 1-in larger all around than your stamp. Carefully brush the fabric paint onto the raised areas of the stamp block, then stamp firmly in the center of one of the linen squares. Lift the block off cleanly, taking care not to smudge the paint. (It may be a good idea to practice this on scrap paper first.)

2 Leave the paint to dry. Some fabric paints need to be pressed on the wrong side with a warm iron to set the paint—check the instructions on the paint pot.

3 When the paint is dry, place the two linen squares together, right sides facing. Pin and stitch a ½-in hem around the top and two sides. Trim the corners. Turn right side out. Stuff the sachet with batting and dried herbs. Turn under and press ½-in on the raw edges, and slipstitch (see page 25, step 6).

4 Sew a colored bead onto each of the corners. If you wish, you could attach a length of ribbon to each top corner so the sachet can be hung around the neck of a coathanger.

# baby's pillow

This pretty mint-green pillow provides a stylish way to warn visitors and family to tread quietly past the nursery. It would make a lovely gift for sleep-deprived new parents wishing to take a nap and make the most of those precious moments when all is quiet and their baby slumbers. During waking hours the pillow can be hung from the end of a newborn baby's cradle or crib.

## YOU WILL NEED

**Ruler or yardstick**

**Scissors**

**Fabric**

**Pins**

**Sewing machine and thread**

**Scrap paper**

**Fabric paint**

**Fine paintbrush**

**Batting**

1 Cut a rectangle of fabric 12 x 18-in. Fold in half crosswise, right sides facing. Pin and stitch a ½-in seam down the two short sides. Trim the corners. Turn right side out and press. The folded edge will be the bottom of the pillow. With a row of pins, mark an inner stitching line 1-in from the bottom and sides, and starting and stopping 1½-in from the open top. Baste along this line, leaving the top open.

## TIP

If you wish, rather than painting a message on the fabric, you could embroider it. Trace the words first with tailor's chalk.

2 Slip a piece of scrap paper inside the pillow, so that the paint does not leak through to the back fabric. Paint your chosen wording within the rectangle marked by the basting. Allow the paint to dry thoroughly. (Some fabric paints need to be pressed with a warm iron to fix them—check the instructions on the paint pot.) Remove the scrap paper.

3 Starting at a point 1½-in from the top edge and one-third of the way along the top, stitch parallel to the top edge, then follow the basting down one side, along the bottom, and up the other side. Continue 1½-in from the top, stopping one-third of the way along the top, so that there is a gap in the center of the top edge. Remove the basting. Stuff the pillow with batting, then neatly stitch the gap closed.

4 To make the hanging strap, cut a piece of fabric 3 x 20-in. Fold the two long edges in toward the center, then fold in half again, so the raw edges are enclosed. Pin together, press, then topstitch. Turn in ½-in on the raw top edges of the back, pin, and press. Slip the two ends of the strap between the front and back edges; pin in place. Slipstitch the top edge closed (see page 25, step 6).

# fabric-covered picture frames

Mismatching picture frames can be given a soft new look by covering them all in a solid-color fabric, with a matching ribbon used instead of picture wire. This is a good way to embellish inexpensive wooden frames. Solid-color fabrics work best as they will not detract from the picture. Choose colors to blend with the artwork you are framing.

## YOU WILL NEED

Plain wooden frame

Paper and pen

Ruler

Scissors

Fabric

White craft glue

Ribbon

Staple gun

## TIP

Choose a heavy, close-weave fabric for this project. This will cover any imperfections in the frame and the glue will not seep through.

1 First, make a pattern for cutting out the fabric. Place the frame on a sheet of paper and draw around it. Draw diagonal lines through the corners.

2 Cut along the diagonal lines to form four pattern pieces. Lay the pattern pieces on the fabric and cut out, adding a ½in seam allowance all around.

3 Smear a thin layer of glue along the front of one side of the frame. Fold under the seam allowance on the diagonal edges of the corresponding piece of fabric and place in position on the frame. Wrap the fabric around the inner and outer edges of the frame, and glue to the back. (You will probably need to trim off some of the fabric to prevent it from becoming too bulky.)

4 Repeat to glue the next piece of fabric in position. Make sure the corners butt up tightly to each other, making a neat miter. Cut some ribbon to the desired length and, using a staple gun, attach it securely to the back of the frame toward the top of the sides.

chapter four

# table linen and accessories

# gathered tablecloth

A generous skirt of gathered pink silk brings a touch of luxury to this entrance hall. This is a neat trick for turning a plain or ugly table into something really special, as the fullness of the cloth hides any horrors lurking beneath the fabric. The cloth is made slightly longer than the table so it can flare out at the base. The top edge of the tablecloth is edged in matching piping for the perfect finishing touch.

## YOU WILL NEED

**Tape measure**

**Scissors**

**Silk or taffeta**

**Pins**

**Sewing machine, with piping foot**

**Needle and thread**

**Piping cord**

## TIP

Do take your time when machine stitching silk or taffeta, as you don't want the threads to pull or the material to buckle under the sewing-machine foot.

1 Measure the tabletop and cut out a circle of fabric to this size plus a ½-in seam allowance all around. Measure and make a note of the tabletop's circumference. Measure and cut out the fabric for the skirt—this needs to be the height of the table plus 4-in, and 1½ times the circumference. Pin the two short edges of the skirt together, right sides facing and taking a ½-in seam allowance. Stitch the seam together and press open.

2 Cut a length of piping cord to the circumference measurement, plus 3-in. To cover the piping, cut a strip of fabric on the bias (diagonal) to the same length and wide enough to wrap around the cord with a ¾-in seam allowance. If you need to join lengths of fabric, join them on the diagonal. Wrap the fabric around the cord, right side out, then machine stitch as close as possible to the cord, using the piping foot.

114

3 Thread the needle with a long piece of thread and sew one or two rows of gathering stitches around the top edge of the skirt, about ½-in from the edge. Gently pull the thread to gather the skirt until it matches the circumference of the table.

4 Place the circular top piece right side up. Pin the piping all around, with the raw edges of the casing fabric facing outward. Clip into the seam allowance of the piping at frequent intervals.

5 To join the piping, unpick the casing fabric on one side and cut away the cord so the two ends butt up. Fold the unpicked casing fabric over the join and trim to ¾-in. Fold under ½-in and pin. Baste the piping in place.

6 Place the skirt on top, wrong side up, with the raw gathered edge even with the edge of the top piece. Pin, taking a ½-in seam allowance. Adjust the gathers so they are even. Stitch. Trim the seam allowances to different widths to make the seam less bulky. Place the cloth on the table and pin a double hem (you can decide how much you want the skirt to flare out). Press and stitch.

# organdy tablecloth

This elegant glass-topped side table boasts two contrasting cloths—an overlong underskirt of fine embroidered cotton topped with an elegant bordered organdy cloth, the sharp angles of the overcloth providing a strong contrast to the flowing lines of the underskirt. These two very different styles can be successfully combined because both cloths contain the same sophisticated shades of gold.

1 Cut the white organdy into a rectangle of the required size, joining pieces with a narrow seam if necessary (but avoiding a central seam). Make a pattern for the border, which has corners with diagonal folds, known as miters. (This is a double-layer border which encloses the edge of the white organdy.) On pattern paper, draw two parallel lines the same length as the long side of the white rectangle, and 11-in apart (these lines mark the front and back seams of the border). Draw a fold line between these two seamlines and extending 5½-in beyond the seamlines at each end. Draw diagonal lines from the ends of the seamlines to the fold line. Add a ½-in seam allowance all around and cut out the pattern.

**TIP**

A glass-topped table such as this would serve equally well as either a drinks table or a dressing table, as the glass protects the fabric from spills.

2 Make another pattern piece the same way for the short side of the rectangle. Pin the pattern pieces to the gold organdy and cut out two short border pieces and two long border pieces.

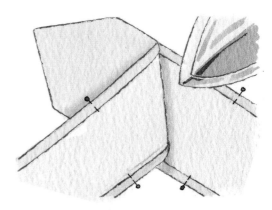

3 Pin one end of a short border to one end of a long border, right sides facing. Stitch a ½-in seam, pivoting at the point and stopping ½-in from each edge. Attach the other two borders in the same way, so all the pointed ends are joined, forming one continuous band. Trim the seams and corners, and turn right side.

4 Turn under, pin, and press a ½-in hem on the front and back edges of the border.

5 With the top and underneath miters aligned at each corner, press from the right side. Sandwich the raw edges of the white rectangle between the border front and back; pin. Stitch all around, along the hemmed inner edge of the border.

6 Pin the narrow white ribbon on top of the seam joining the white and gold organdy. Stitch in place along both edges, folding it neatly at the corners.

# scallop-edged tablecloth

Made in classic kitchen colors of blue and white, this fitted linen tablecloth has a decorative scalloped edge trimmed with navy blue piping. Here the scallops have been cut from blue-and-white dish towels in a mixture of checks and stripes. As the cloth is made to fit snugly around the table, it would be a good idea to launder all the fabrics before cutting and stitching them together, just in case of shrinkage.

## YOU WILL NEED

Tape measure

Heavy cream linen

Navy blue bias binding (see step 2)

Scissors

Sewing machine, with piping foot

Thread

Piping cord

Pins

Pattern paper

Selection of blue-and-white dish towels

## TIP

This scalloped tablecloth would look extremely stylish used with the simple plaid slipcovers featured on page 60.

1 Measure the tabletop and cut out a circle of linen to this size, plus a ½-in seam allowance all around. For the side piece, measure the circumference of the table and cut out a rectangle of linen to this length plus 1-in, and with a depth of 6-in.

2 For the bias binding, cut a length of navy fabric on the bias (diagonal), as long as the circumference of the table, plus 1-in, and wide enough to wrap around the cord with a ½-in seam allowance. If you need to join lengths of fabric, join them on the diagonal. For the piping, wrap the bias binding around the cord, right side out. Machine stitch as close to the cord as possible, using the piping foot.

3 To make the scallops, first cut a paper pattern. Draw the desired scallop shape onto pattern paper (it may be easiest to draw halfway around a dinner plate and extend the sides). Allow a ½-in seam allowance all around. Make sure that the width of the scallop will allow you to edge the cloth with complete scallops without any gaps between them.

4 For each
scallop, cut out
two pieces of
dish-towel fabric.
Pin them together,
right sides facing and
taking a ½-in seam. Stitch
around the sides and curved bottom of each
scallop. Clip into the curves within the seam
allowance, then turn right side out, and press.

5 Pin the piping to the right side of the
linen rectangle, with the seam allowance facing
outward. Pin the scallops in place, with the
curved bottoms facing inward and making sure
the different patterns are evenly spaced.
Sew in place.

6 Pin the two ends of the scallop-edged rectangle
together, right sides facing, taking a ½-in seam. Stitch
together from the top down as far as the piping. When
you reach the piping, unpick a few stitches on the fabric
casing at each end, and trim the cord so both ends butt
together neatly. Fold the fabric casing neatly to enclose the
cord and hand-sew together. Press the seam flat.

7 Pin the scalloped side edging to the linen
circle, right sides facing and raw edges even. Clip
into the seam allowance at frequent intervals.
Stitch a ½-in seam, and press.

# linen
# silverware roll

This stylish linen roll is perfect for storing or transporting flatware. Use it for picnics, or store special-occasion knives and forks in it. You can alter the measurements to make it as large or small as you wish—for a picnic you could make individual sleeves for each place setting, and include a pocket for a napkin. The pocket widths can also be adapted—stitch wide ones for spoons and serving implements, and narrower ones for knives and forks.

**YOU WILL NEED**

**Yardstick**

**Scissors**

**Linen**

**Pins**

**Sewing machine and thread**

1 Cut a rectangle of linen 20 x 15-in for the backing. Cut a second rectangle 7 x 15-in for the pocket. Fold over, pin, and stitch a ½-in hem along one long edge of the smaller rectangle— this will be the top edge of the pocket.

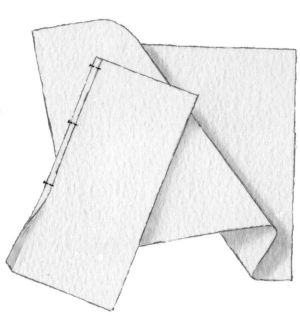

**TIP**

If you wish, make the pocket and backing each 4-in deeper, so the backing can be folded over before the linen is rolled up, to safeguard the contents completely.

2 Place the smaller rectangle on top of the large rectangle, with its long raw edge matching one of the short raw edges of the large piece and with the hem facing inward. Both pieces should be right side up. Pin, then baste the pocket to the backing piece.

3 Fold the large rectangle in half, so the pocket is enclosed on the inside. Pin the side seams, then stitch a ½-in seam. Trim the corners, remove the basting, then turn right side out. Press.

4 Turn in ½-in along the lower raw edges and pin. Topstitch all around the outer edge of the backing piece.

6 To make a tie, cut a rectangle of linen 3 x 15-in. Turn under and press ¼-in on all the raw edges, then fold this in half lengthwise and pin. Topstitch all around the edges. Fold the tie in half to find the center point, then pin the tie halfway up one of the short edges. Stitch firmly through the center of the tie. Insert the flatware in the pocket sections, roll up the linen, and secure with the tie.

5 Decide on the width of the individual pockets and then mark the stitching lines with pins. Stitch along the marked lines, stopping at the top edge of the pocket.

# index

## author's acknowledgments

Many thanks to Christine Wood for her elegant design and for all her support.
Thank you to Kate Simunek for translating my instructions into such
beautiful artworks. And a big thank you to Cindy Richards,
Alison Wormleighton and Corinne Asghar and all at Cico Books.